JESUS
SANG
ON THE
CROSS

DR. RANDY T. JOHNSON

First Edition, January 2020

Published by:
The River Church
8393 E. Holly Rd.
Holly, MI 48442

Scriptures are taken from the Bible,
New International Version (UK)

Printed in the United States of America

CONTENTS

INTRODUCTION

I was raised with a very simple philosophy:

> God said it.
> I believe it.
> That settles it.

This mantra appears to be sound as we work our way through the Children's Church and into Youth Group. However, once we step out of our Church setting and onto the college campus or into the workplace, people want proof.

One of the greatest pitfalls facing Christian teens stepping into the next stage of life is that they do not know why they believe what they believe. Most Christians are not raised in a setting that allows "tough" questions. They do not know why they can trust the Bible.

I was told about a college professor who would start each semester by ridiculing the Bible and anyone who believed in it. He would announce how it was not trustworthy as it was full of errors. Finally, one semester, a student approached the professor after the class. He asked, "Can you point out one of the supposed errors in the Bible?" The professor quickly replied, "The Bible records two sets of Ten Commandments, and they contradict each other."

How would you have responded?

Are there two sets of Ten Commandments?

If so, do they contradict each other?

This student was prepared. He knew that the second pair of tablets needed to be created because Moses broke the first set (It can be said that Moses is the most sinful man of all time as he "broke" all Ten Commandments in less than five seconds). The two sets are recorded in Exodus chapter 20 and Deuteronomy chapter 5. However, they do not contradict each other as they are identical. The professor had heard someone say there were errors, he wanted to believe that, and so without confirmation, he accepted the statement as truth. Unfortunately, he then spread the lie.

The Bible is amazing. The more you read, study, and meditate on it, you will be awed by its depth that reaches into your daily life.

There are so many fun facts about the Bible:

- Written on three different continents.
- It originally contained three different languages.
- It took at least 40 authors.
- They wrote over a period of over 1500 years.
- It was first translated into English by John Wycliffe in 1382.
- It was the first book ever produced on a printing press (1454). Johannes Gutenberg, who invented the "type mold" for the printing press, chose the Bible as his first and primary document.
- It is the best seller of all time.
- Over five billion copies of the Bible have been sold (not counting apps).

Jesus Sang on the Cross will help strengthen your faith in the truth and power of God's Word. It will also prove that Jesus is the Messiah, the Savior.

CHAPTER 1
ONE OF A KIND

What makes the Bible special or unique?

Pause and think about that question for a moment.

If you answered, "It is God's Word," you are right, but just about everyone has a book they refer to as God's Word. Maybe you thought, "It is true." Again, you are right, but so is a second-grade math book. It is more than that. Or you might have calmly and confidently said, "The Bible changed my life." I, too, know from experience how that can be true, yet the Bible is more than just a self-help book. Books can change lives, but the Bible goes much further.

The Bible is special and unique in that it not only accurately records the past, but tells the future. Several of these prophecies have already happened with more yet to come.

Jesus Sang on the Cross will clearly prove how one can trust the Bible as God's only written Word. In doing this, it will also show that Jesus was and is the Messiah. A careful study of Psalm chapter 22 reveals prophecy that was fulfilled by Jesus' death. It was not a story involving only one person as several enemies (guards, soldiers, criminals, priests, and by-standers) of Jesus also participated in proving God's Word is true, and Jesus is His Son.

Psalm chapter 22 has at least ten specific words, phrases, or actions that were accomplished 1,000 years later at the crucifixion of Jesus Christ.

Psalm Chapter 22:

> For the director of music.
> To the tune of **'The Doe of the Morning'.**
> **A psalm of David.**

1 **My God, my God, why have you forsaken me?**
  Why are you so far from saving me, so far from my
  cries of anguish?
2 My God, I cry out by day, but you do not answer,
  by night, but I find no rest.
3 Yet you are enthroned as the Holy One; you are the
  one Israel praises.
4 In you our ancestors put their trust;
  they trusted and you delivered them.
5 To you they cried out and were saved;
  in you they trusted and were not put to shame.
6 But I am a worm and not a man,
  scorned by everyone, **despised** by the people.
7 All who see me **mock** me; they **hurl** insults, **shaking
  their heads.**
8 'He trusts in the Lord,' they say, **'let the Lord rescue
  him.**
  Let him deliver him, since he delights in him.'
9 Yet you brought me out of the womb;
  you made me trust in you, even at my mother's breast.
10 From birth I was cast on you;
  from my mother's womb you have been my God.
11 Do not be far from me, for trouble is near and there is
  no one to help.
12 Many **bulls** surround me; strong bulls of Bashan
  encircle me.

¹³ Roaring **lions** that tear their prey open their mouths wide against me.

¹⁴ I am poured out like water, and all my **bones are out of joint.**
My heart has turned to wax; it has melted within me.

¹⁵ **My mouth is dried up** like a potsherd, and my tongue sticks to the roof of my mouth; you lay me in the **dust of death.**

¹⁶ **Dogs** surround me, a pack of villains encircles me; they **pierce my hands and my feet.**

¹⁷ All my **bones are on display;** people stare and gloat over me.

¹⁸ They **divide my clothes** among them and **cast lots for my garment.**

¹⁹ But you, Lord, do not be far from me.
You are my strength; come quickly to help me.

²⁰ Deliver me from the sword,
my **precious life** from the power of the **dogs.**

²¹ Rescue me from the mouth of the **lions;**
save me from the horns of the **wild oxen.**

²² I will declare your name to my people;
in the assembly I will praise you.

²³ You who fear the Lord, praise him! All you descendants of Jacob, honour him! Revere him, all you descendants of Israel!

²⁴ For **he** has not despised or scorned the suffering of the **afflicted one;**
he has not hidden ʜɪꜱ face from **him** but has listened to **his** cry for help.

²⁵ From **you** comes the theme of my praise in the great assembly;
before those who **fear you** I will **fulfil my vows.**

[26] The poor will eat and be satisfied; those who **seek the Lord** will praise him – **may your hearts live forever!**

[27] All the ends of the earth will remember and turn to the Lord,
and all the families of the nations will bow down before him,

[28] for dominion belongs to the Lord and he rules over the nations.

[29] All the rich of the earth will feast and worship;
all who go down to the dust will kneel before him –
those who cannot keep themselves alive.

[30] Posterity will serve him;
future generations will be told about the Lord.

[31] They will proclaim his righteousness,
declaring to a people yet unborn: **He has done it!**

CHAPTER 2
FORSAKEN

My God, my God,
why have you forsaken me?
Why are you so far from saving me,
so far from my cries of anguish?

Psalm 22:1

Jesus spoke at least seven last statements from the cross. Six of them are understood pretty straight forward; however, one deserves more discussion and insight.

Matthew 27:46 records, *"About three in the afternoon Jesus cried out in a loud voice, 'Eli, Eli, lema sabachthani?' (which means 'My God, my God, why have you forsaken me?')."* Mark 15:34 also records the scenario.

Why does Jesus say, *"My God, My God, why have you forsaken me?"* There are two major yet different interpretations of why Jesus bellowed this phrase.

1. Jesus was confused and abandoned.

Dr. Paul Perkins wrote a book specifically on Psalm chapter 22, entitled, *"Refrain of Silence."* In his book, he says, "'My God, My God! Why have you forsaken me?' The first line of Psalm 22 are the same words slipping through the blood-stained lips of Jesus on the cross. 'Father, Father! Why are you not listening?' Nothing. No booming voices saying, 'This is my son whom I am well pleased.' No moment of chastisement from heaven that said, 'This is my Son, listen to Him.' No heavenly vision of a dove descending on His brow. No angel comforting Him as in the wilderness or the garden. Nothing! At the moment the weight of God's wrath was laid on His shoulders, and for the first time, EVER, the Father turned His back on the Son!"

As is commonly held, Dr. Perkins says God abandoned Jesus. The Father could not look on His Son because of our sin. His holiness could not receive the filth of our sin. Jesus carried the filth; the Father turned His back. Miles Custis adds, "Jesus' physical sufferings pale in comparison to the trauma of being forsaken by God as he takes the weight of our sin upon himself."

This view has several dangerous outcomes. First, it comes across as if Jesus is confused. Was Jesus confused? Did He not understand what was happening? Did Jesus understand He would carry the weight of everyone's sin?

Matthew chapter 26 describes Jesus' psyche before He climbed onto the cross as He was at the Garden of Gethsemane. Verse 39 says, ***"Going a little farther, he fell with his face to the ground and prayed, 'My Father, if it is possible, may this cup be taken from me. Yet not as I will, but as you will.'"***

Jesus knew what He was facing. He was not confused. He came to Earth with one mission in mind – bridge the gap between God and man that was caused by man's sin. Verses 40-41 record that the disciples kept falling asleep. Jesus wanted them to witness His conversation with the Father so that they would realize there was no other way for man to be restored to God.

Finally, verse 42 says, ***"He went away a second time and prayed, 'My Father, if it is not possible for this cup to be taken away unless I drink it, may your will be done.'"***

Second, this view depicts a God who abandons. If God can abandon His Only Son, then maybe He will abandon us.

Vance Royal Olson boldly addresses this viewpoint, "Unfortunately, somewhere in the history of the Church and theology, a superficial interpretation of this 'cry of dereliction' or 'word of despair,' as it has variously been called, led to a

terrible heresy that has all but obscured the meaning of the whole Psalm. The heresy – and it is one of the most insidious of all time – is that the Father abandoned Jesus, in his darkest hour and moment of deepest need, on the cross."

He goes on to mention that the message of the cross declares the opposite of abandonment. In the Garden after Adam and Eve sinned, God came looking for them. He did not leave them or give up on them. He saw them with their sin and immediately provided a means for reconciliation (Genesis 3:15). The sin of Adam and Eve is recorded in Genesis chapter 3, and before you even turn the page, God provided a means for salvation. Sin has consequences; God provides a means to salvation. Instead of turning His back, God reached out with His hand.

John 16:32 addresses this concern, *"A time is coming and in fact has come when you will be scattered, each to your own home. You will leave me all alone. Yet I am not alone, for my Father is with me."*

Jesus was not confused, and God did not abandon Him.

Billy Graham had so many words of comfort, "God didn't abandon Jesus, and He won't abandon you. Make Him part of your life today."

If Jesus was not confused and God did not abandon Him, then why did He say, *"My God, My God, why have you forsaken me?"* From studying Psalm chapter 22, it is clear why He asked the question, or more accurately, made a statement.

2. Jesus was fulfilling prophecy.

As Jesus was finishing His mission, He figuratively pulled out a hymnal and had everyone turn to the page containing Psalm chapter 22. He then began the song, *"My God, my God, why have you forsaken me?"* Others would have joined. There were not many copies of Scripture available, and many of the common folk were illiterate. However, every Hebrew male thirteen and older had memorized the Torah (the first five books of the Old Testament) and the Psalms. They knew the Psalm.

Just as a rabbi would start a portion of Scripture and his students would finish it, so did Jesus. The Master Teacher began the song, and the Hebrew crowd continued it. Some may have softly sung it, others may have hummed the passage, but all had the words flow through their mind.

The script for the crucifixion of the Messiah was now playing out before their very eyes. It now began to make sense.

To be even more pointed with His message, Jesus broke away from the Greek and spoke in Aramaic. It is the only phrase where He chose to target a specific audience. He said, *"Eli, Eli, lema sabachthani?"* He spoke to the Jews, taking them back 1,000 years to a writing by David. It must have been mind-blowing. Jesus was and is the Messiah. He is the Savior.

Roger Ellsworth in his book, *Opening Up Psalms,* says it so well, "Here, David lifts up his eyes, looks down the long corridor of time, and sees in striking detail the crucifixion of the Messiah who was yet to come."

In contrast to those who think David is speaking about his own life, H.D.M. Spence-Jones says, "We have to call this a psalm of prophecy—even as the apostle Peter referred to Psalm 132 as a psalm of prophecy (Acts 2:30–31)—because we can find nothing in David's life that would require the language he uses in these verses and because we do find the cross of Christ answering detail after detail of the psalm. Some have suggested that this prediction of the cross is so exact that it makes us think it had to be written by one standing at the foot of the cross. But this is not the psalm of an observer reporting an event. It was written almost a thousand years before the event, and it is written in the first person. Here we have one telling about his own experience. We have to say, therefore, that this psalm is the result of the Spirit of God taking over the pen of David in a strange and marvelous way so he, David, was able to write the very words of the Messiah himself."

David was not writing about his own life. It was prophecy about the promised Messiah. Several of the items in this narrative were never experienced by David. Spence-Jones goes on to say, "He was never without a helper (ver. 11); never 'despised of the people' (ver. 6); never stripped of his clothes (ver. 17); never in the state of exhaustion, weakness, and emaciation that are spoken of (vers. 14–17); never pierced either in his hands or feet (ver. 16); never made a gazing-stock (ver. 17); never insulted by having his garments parted among his persecutors, or lots cast upon his vesture (ver. 18)."

There are at least twelve references made in Psalm chapter 22 that find their origination ten centuries later as Jesus hung on a cross.

CHAPTER 3

"MY GOD, MY GOD, WHY HAVE YOU FORSAKEN ME?"

For the director of music.
To the tune of
'The Doe of the Morning.'
A psalm of David.
My God, my God,
why have you forsaken me?
Why are you so far from saving me,
so far from my cries of anguish?

Psalm 22:1

Movie lines can be so fascinating. They can soften a tense moment or clarify a point in a subtle way. Hearing a quote from a movie can take you right back to the emotions you experienced when you first heard it. Great movie lines come in a variety of genres. A few examples are:

"Fish are friends, not food."
Finding Nemo, 2003

"Show me the money."
Jerry Maguire, 1996

"Mama says, 'Stupid is as stupid does.'"
Forrest Gump, 1994

"So you're telling me there's a chance!"
Dumb and Dumber, 1994

"You can't handle the truth!"
A Few Good Men, 1992

"Carpe diem. Seize the day, boys."
Dead Poets Society, 1989

"If you build it, they will come."
Field of Dreams, 1989

"I'll be back."
The Terminator, 1984

"May the force be with you."
Star Wars, 1977

"I'm going to make him an offer he can't refuse."
The Godfather, 1972

"You've got to ask yourself one question: 'Do I feel lucky?'
Well, do ya punk?"
Dirty Harry, 1971

"Here's looking at you, kid."
Casablanca, 1942

"There's no place like home."
The Wizard of Oz, 1939

Hopefully, an emotion of warmth puts a smile on your face.

David kind of wrote the powerful "movie" line before the action took place. He wrote, **"My God, my God, why have you forsaken me?"** Either Jesus was quoting David or David was quoting Jesus 1,000 years earlier.

This similarity between Psalm chapter 22 and Jesus' crucifixion cannot be overlooked or overemphasized. Emotions should be stirred.

Psalm 22:1 starts off by saying, **"My God, my God, why have you forsaken me?"** This is the exact phrase used by Jesus on the cross. The reader has to ask, "Why did David write this?" The listener has to ask, "Why did Jesus say or quote this?" Looking back, we have the advantage of answering both questions.

David's Life

David's life had many stages. He had quiet time with glimpses of heroism as a shepherd, celebration moments in the aftermath of his combat with Goliath, times of hysteria with King Saul, nights where he slept in a cave with one eye open, and nights where he was massaged until he fell asleep in the castle. The Psalms are full of emotions. He worships God, yet at times, he feels all alone.

You can have people all around you and still feel all alone. David experienced this. So, is that why he says, *"My God, my God, why have you forsaken me? Why are you so far from saving me, so far from my cries of anguish?"*

Miles Custis says, "The opening line of Psalm 22 beautifully expresses the anguish of the psalmist. He is suffering greatly, but his chief concern is that God—the source of his trust and deliverance—appears to have abandoned him." He is right, and the application of turning to God in times of trouble preaches well. However, his view is shallow and short-sighted. Even John Calvin noted, "David, therefore, complains that God is in a manner deaf to his prayers. When he says in the second clause, *And there is no silence to me,* the meaning is, that he experienced no comfort or solace, nothing which could impart tranquility to his troubled mind."

David did have trying times, but much more is going on here.

Allen Ross wrote in *The Bible Knowledge Commentary,* "No known incident in the life of David fits the details of this psalm. The expressions describe an execution, not an illness; yet, that execution is more appropriate to Jesus' crucifixion than David's experience." This is the point of the psalm.

Jesus' Death

Charles Spurgeon is very straightforward in his view calling Psalm chapter 22, "The Psalm of the Cross." Spurgeon says, "This is beyond all others THE PSALM OF THE CROSS. It may have been actually repeated word by word by our Lord when hanging on the tree."

Bradley W. Maston adds, "Many great theologians have even believed that Christ prayed this Psalm as His prayer throughout the entire ordeal of the crucifixion."

This is an amazing concept to consider. Jesus could have said more things while on the cross. Not one of the Gospel writers (Matthew, Mark, Luke, and John) documented all seven sayings. They wrote what was most applicable for their targeted audience by the direction of the Holy Spirit.

Jesus could have said more things. He could have quoted the whole psalm from a bird's eye view on the cross while watching it play out all around him. Either way, His Hebrew (Aramaic speaking) audience heard His words, they continued the song, and if they were observant at all, they saw different actors taking their part in fulfilling this passage.

It is mind-blowing to think of what Jesus needed to do to speak. Jesus' chest cavity was collapsing. Each breath was savored, hoping for another. He pushed up from the spike through His feet and pulled from His wounded hands just to release the pressure on the lungs long enough to swallow some air. With this all in mind, how did He spend that valued air? He provided for His mother and a friend. He offered forgiveness and then took everyone back 1,000 years to a writing attributed to King David.

Each of the seven phrases is important. He fought forward to declare what needed to be said. In His final breaths, He was still intentionally providing for others. He knew His mission, and it was and is of utmost importance that everyone else realized it.

Side Note

Psalm chapter 22 actually starts, *"For the director of music. To the tune of 'The Doe of the Morning.' A psalm of David."* Most people view these words as a summary statement or subscript. However, it is actually verse one in the Hebrew Bible.

From this verse, we know the author is David. Archeology and a historical timeline have taught that David lived from about 1040 – 960 BC. This can become more important later as some skeptics have challenged the age of this psalm. They assume it must have been written at the time of Christ as the details are so precise. The criticism is actually encouraging as it again points to the power and uniqueness of the Holy Bible.

Within these opening lines, we read about *"The Doe of the Morning."* Some scholars have wondered if the *"Doe"* was a reference to an animal sacrifice, highlighting Jesus as the Ultimate Sacrifice. Furthermore, they have quoted Revelation 22:16, showing the *"Morning"* reference as a title for Jesus, *"I, Jesus, have sent my angel to give you this testimony for the churches. I am the Root and the Offspring of David, and the bright Morning Star."*

These are interesting observations, but I do not list them as some of the primary points directing our attention to the cross of Jesus. These are merely viewed as sub-points. There are some very compelling arguments that, in essence, advance the Gospel.

Practical Side

The bottom line is that no matter how lonely David felt, and no matter how similar parts of David's life related, this Psalm points to Jesus. Charles Spurgeon was very practical when he said, "For plaintive expressions uprising from unutterable depths of woe we may say of this psalm, 'there is none like it.' It is the photograph of our Lord's saddest hours, the record of his dying words, the lachrymatory of his last tears, the memorial of his expiring joys. David and his afflictions may be here in a very modified sense, but, as the star is concealed by the light of the sun, he who sees Jesus will probably neither see nor care to see David."

Jesus is seen in this Psalm. There are at least eleven other references that prove this point.

CHAPTER 4
MOCKED

But I am a worm and not a man,
scorned by everyone, despised by the people.
All who see me mock me;
they hurl insults, shaking their heads.
'He trusts in the Lord,' they say, 'let the
Lord rescue him. Let him deliver him,
since he delights in him.'
Yet you brought me out of the womb;
you made me trust in you, even at my
mother's breast.
From birth I was cast on you; from my
mother's womb you have been my God.
Do not be far from me, for trouble is near
and there is no one to help.

Psalm 22:6-11

One of the toughest lines that children are taught to say goes something like this, "Sticks and stones may break my bones, but names will never hurt me." It sure sounds simple, but words can pierce the inner core for years to come. Injuries heal, but a broken heart does not show up on an x-ray.

Another similarity between Psalm chapter 22 and Jesus' crucifixion is found in verse seven and is also very obvious.

Psalm chapter 22 is describing the promised Messiah. It would not make sense to the original readers that the Messiah would be mocked. They were expecting a mighty, victorious leader. When the Messiah came (Jesus), He was that, but many could not see it.

Jesus was mocked

Psalm 22:6-8 says, *"But I am a worm and not a man, scorned by everyone, despised by the people. All who see me mock me; they hurl insults, shaking their heads. 'He trusts in the Lord,' they say, 'let the Lord rescue him. Let him deliver him, since he delights in him.'"*

David was not mocked. He was a hero and a king. Even while he was on the run, he had a full entourage with him. He was not mocked. People were not hurling insults at him. However, they did to Jesus.

Matthew 27:39-43 records some of the events while Jesus hung on the cross, *"Those who passed by hurled insults at him, shaking their heads and saying, 'You who are going to destroy the temple and build it in three days, save yourself! Come down from the cross, if you are the Son of God!' In the same way the chief priests, the teachers of the law and the elders mocked him. 'He saved others,' they said, 'but he can't save himself! He's the king of Israel! Let him come down now from the cross, and we will believe in him. He trusts in God. Let God rescue him now if he wants him, for he said, 'I am the Son of God.''*

It is amazing how similar the passages match each other.

Matthew 27	Psalm 22
"Hurled insults" v. 39	*"They hurl insults"* v. 7
"Shaking their heads" v. 39	*"Shaking their heads"* v. 7
"Mocked him" v. 41	*"Mock me"* v. 7
"He trusts in God.	*"He trusts in the Lord,*
Let God rescue him." v. 43	*Let the Lord rescue him."* v. 8

In the first example of the similarities of Psalm chapter 22 and Jesus' crucifixion, Jesus quoted this psalm in saying, *"My God, my God, why have you forsaken me?"* Critics could try to diffuse the power of this observation in saying that Jesus "forced" the situation. He chose to fulfill that prophecy by saying those words. Their point is well-taken, but what about all these statements? Jesus' enemies made these statements. The ones who a few hours earlier were shouting, "Crucify Him," have continued their vocal rage. In essence, they are helping Jesus fulfill prophecy. By denying He was the Messiah, they fulfilled a prophecy on how the Messiah would be treated.

Isaiah 53:3 says, *"He was despised and rejected by mankind, a man of suffering, and familiar with pain. Like one from whom people hide their faces he was despised, and we held him in low esteem."* Isaiah wrote some 700 years before Jesus saying that the Messiah would be despised and rejected. The word despised is even used twice in the verse. It is clear that David and Isaiah were referring to the Messiah (Jesus).

It is impressive that even though Jesus was being mocked, He remained silent. He did not get into a battle of words. It was another great example for us. John Wooden has said, "Be more concerned with your character than your reputation, because your character is what you really are, while your reputation is merely what others think you are." Jesus knew He was God. He knew He was innocent. However, He also knew He needed to die for us.

Side Note

There is another observation from Psalm chapter 22 that can relate to Jesus throughout His life and death. Psalm 22:6 says, ***"But I am a worm and not a man, scorned by everyone, despised by the people."*** Jesus is referred to as a worm. It does not get much lower than that of being a worm.

Philippians 2:5-8 answers the question of how low Jesus was willing to go, ***"In your relationships with one another, have the same mindset as Christ Jesus: who, being in very nature God, did not consider equality with God something to be used to his own advantage; rather, he made himself nothing by taking the very nature of a servant, being made in human likeness. And being found in appearance as a man, he humbled himself by becoming obedient to death – even death on a cross!"***

Jesus was and is God. Even though He was God, He emptied Himself by making Himself ***"nothing."*** As if that was not low enough, He took the appearance of a man, died, and even died on a cross. That is how low He was willing to go for us.

Not only was Jesus' death one of humility, but His daily walk also displayed it. Even though He could have chosen to look any way He wanted, He did not choose to be striking. Isaiah 53:2 says, *"He grew up before him like a tender shoot, and like a root out of dry ground. He had no beauty or majesty to attract us to him, nothing in his appearance that we should desire him."* The Bible refers to the beauty of Joseph and David, but not of Jesus. *"He had no beauty or majesty to attract us to him."* He did not choose the high road.

"I am a worm" is another subtle similarity between Psalm chapter 22 and the crucifixion of Jesus.

Another Side Note

Psalm 22:9-11 continues the passage, *"Yet you brought me out of the womb; you made me trust in you, even at my mother's breast. From birth I was cast on you; from my mother's womb you have been my God. Do not be far from me, for trouble is near and there is no one to help."*

Jesus was on a mission. Even when He was in Mary's womb, He and God already had a plan. Mark 10:45 says, *"For even the Son of Man did not come to be served, but to serve, and to give his life as a ransom for many."* From the womb, birth, and while being nursed, Jesus was called to a mission. He chose to come to Earth to fulfill a promise that was a mission impossible for everyone else.

Practical Side

There are two beautiful applications that are good to remember as we read through Psalm chapter 22.

First, just as God and Jesus had a plan for His life, God has a plan for our lives. Jeremiah 1:4-5 says, *"The word of the Lord came to me, saying, 'Before I formed you in the womb I knew you, before you were born I set you apart; I appointed you as a prophet to the nations.'"* God knows us even before we are born. He has a plan for our lives. Jeremiah also wrote, *"'For I know the plans I have for you,' declares the Lord, 'plans to prosper you and not to harm you, plans to give you hope and a future'"* (29:11). Seek God. Follow the Lord. Live the plan.

Second, as David writes Psalm chapter 22, he makes a powerful notation. In verse 9, he writes, *"Yet you."* He makes the same kind of reference in verse 19, *"But you, Lord."* Throughout the commotion and devastation of the cross, Jesus knew God was present. Likewise, the world may come against us or be falling apart all around us. Remember, that no matter how bad the odds seem, there is the "but God" factor. He can always step in and overrule any situation. He is in control. We may not know what the future holds, but we know Who holds the future.

Jesus grabbed the attention of every Aramaic speaking person with the opening line of Psalm chapter 22. As they listened to Him quote the rest of the passage, or as they mouthed the words themselves, they watched the whole picture come into focus. He was mocked and despised by many differing groups.

CHAPTER 5
EVIL MEN ALL AROUND HIM

Many bulls surround me; strong bulls of
Bashan encircle me.
Roaring lions that tear their prey open their
mouths wide against me.

Psalm 22:12-13

Martin Luther King, Jr. wisely said, "An eye for an eye leaves everybody blind." Dr. King strived for peace. He also said, "Nonviolence is the answer to the crucial political and moral questions of our time: the need for man to overcome oppression and violence without resorting to oppression and violence. Man must evolve for all human conflict a method which rejects revenge, aggression, and retaliation. The foundation of such a method is love." Even though he and those with him were being treated cruelly, he encouraged his people to not strike back with a fist, tongue, or from the heart (hatred).

With evil men all around Him, Jesus chose love. This is described in Psalm chapter 22 and seen at the crucifixion of Jesus. It may not seem very profound, but no one expected the Messiah to have evil people all around Him.

Psalm 22:12-13 says, *"Many bulls surround me; strong bulls of Bashan encircle me. Roaring lions that tear their prey open their mouths wide against me."* Verse 16 adds, *"Dogs surround me, a pack of villains encircles me; they pierce my hands and my feet."*

Most commentators speak of the bulls (v. 12), lions (v. 13), and dogs (v. 16) as representative of the enemies of Christ. Vance Olson believes they may even imply or refer to the many evil spirits that were present at the crucifixion. Either way, evil was all around the Savior as He hung on the cross.

Bulls are to be feared. Most people know you do not mess with bulls, or you will get the horns. Lions make great symbols and crests but are a paralyzing threat when encountered in the wild. Finally, dogs were scavengers. They carried diseases and were known to run in packs as they filtered through garbage and decaying road kill. This was not a loyal family pet. It was the local nuisance and predator.

David's reference to bulls, lions, and dogs was not intended to bring back fond childhood memories of the family picnic at the local zoo. It was a fierce situation. It reeked of death and destruction.

He was surrounded by evil individuals and was even crucified between two criminals. Theses rebels strained their muscles as they pushed from the nail through their feet and pulled in excruciating pain from the nails through their hands. They endured this just so they could relieve the pressure from their lungs, gulp some air, and speak against the innocent one next to them. It is amazing to see how they wasted their last few breathes. Fortunately, one of the criminals next to Jesus saw his folly and changed his ways, his words, and his destiny.

Isaiah 53:9 points out some interesting points about the Messiah, *"He was assigned a grave with the wicked, and with the rich in his death, though he had done no violence, nor was any deceit in his mouth."* Jesus was crucified and died with *"the wicked."* By the way, He did end up *"with the rich in his death."*

John 19:38-42 speaks about a rich man offering his tomb to be used for Jesus, *"Later, Joseph of Arimathea asked Pilate for the body of Jesus. Now Joseph was a disciple of Jesus, but secretly because he feared the Jewish leaders. With Pilate's permission, he came and took the body away. He was accompanied by Nicodemus, the man who earlier had visited Jesus at night. Nicodemus brought a mixture of myrrh and aloes, about thirty-five kilograms.*

Taking Jesus' body, the two of them wrapped it, with the spices, in strips of linen. This was in accordance with Jewish burial customs. At the place where Jesus was crucified, there was a garden, and in the garden a new tomb, in which no one had ever been laid. Because it was the Jewish day of Preparation and since the tomb was near by, they laid Jesus there." Joseph of Arimathea and Nicodemus were wealthy men who came to handle the dead body of Jesus properly. Joseph gave his tomb for the Messiah. Jesus did end up *"with the rich in his death."* It was only needed for three days.

Psalm chapter 22 refers to one being surrounded by evil men who want to devour and tear one apart. This is not a reference to David, but Jesus and His crucifixion.

CHAPTER 5: EVIL MEN ALL AROUND HIM

CHAPTER 6
HEART TURNED
TO WAX

I am poured out like water,
and all my bones are out of joint.
My heart has turned to wax:
it has melted within me.

Psalm 22:14

The Mayo Clinic is top-ranked for quality more often than any other health care organization in the world. The *U.S. News & World Report* always ranks them as one of the best if not the very best hospital in a number of fields of study. Unfortunately, many know about Mayo Clinic because they or a family member have exhausted all local solutions to a health problem, so they traveled to a Mayo Clinic. Needless to say, they are a reliable source.

Josh McDowell said that the Mayo Clinic documented that Psalm 22:14 describes a crucifixion. The verse says, ***"I am poured out like water, and all my bones are out of joint. My heart has turned to wax; it has melted within me."***

This is an amazing statement. The physical trauma described in this verse points past David and even David's time. It points to a crucifixion.

What makes this even more amazing is that no one was crucified during David's lifetime. They used other means of execution.

In Joshua chapter 7, we read about the sin of Achan. When Israel had defeated Jericho, God told them not to take any of the possessions. However, Achan did. He hid them in his tent. Israel lost the next battle to a small town named Ai. They were confused. Achan's sin was the problem. It was revealed and had to be handled. He was sentenced to be executed. Crucifixion was not "invented" yet. They stoned Achan.

In the book of Esther, Haman despises Mordecai for not worshiping him. He makes plans for a public execution. He wants to make a statement to everyone. Unfortunately, his "vehicle" of execution was later used on him. Esther 7:9 records, *"Then Harbona, one of the eunuchs attending the king, said, 'A pole reaching to a height of fifty cubits stands by Haman's house. He had it set up for Mordecai, who spoke up to help the king.' The king said, 'Impale him on it!'"* Crucifixion was not an option. It had not been chosen or thought of yet.

Actually, Psalm chapter 22 describes a crucifixion 800 years before the Romans put this means of execution into practice.

It is mind-boggling to realize that David writes of Jesus' crucifixion while not even knowing what one was. He wrote this 1,000 years before Jesus' death.

Again, verse 14 says, *"I am poured out like water, and all my bones are out of joint. My heart has turned to wax; it has melted within me."* It is clear that when they took His body that was lying on the cross, picked it up, and dumped it in a hole, His body would have been severely jarred. The pressure could dislocate the shoulders. The added strain just to take a breath could allow for Him saying, *"All my bones are out of joint."*

Ed Rickard wrote, "The grotesque stretching of His arms and cramping of His legs as Jesus hung on the cross must truly have produced a sensation of extreme pressure on His joints. It is possible that in a typical crucifixion, the victim's arms were attached to the patibulum before it was lifted onto the stipes. Perhaps the pull on Jesus' arms as He was yanked off the ground actually dislocated His shoulders."

Furthermore, the Mayo Clinic described how the lungs would fill with water making it feel like his heart had turned to wax and was melting within Him.

The heart being turned to wax is only the fourth of at least twelve similarities of Psalm chapter 22 and the crucifixion of Jesus. Due to the Mayo Clinic documentation, it is probably the only evidence needed, but there are many more fascinating points to examine.

CHAPTER 6: HEART TURNED TO WAX

CHAPTER 7
THIRSTY

My mouth is dried up like a potsherd,
and my tongue sticks to the roof of my mouth;
you lay me in the dust of death.

Psalm 22:15

Beauty and Tips wrote an article entitled "10 interesting facts about water." The list includes:

1. You can get drunk on water.
2. You need water more than you need food.
3. Did you know that hot water freezes faster than cold?
4. It is easy to become dehydrated.
5. Depression and fatigue can be brought on by a lack of water.
6. Water doesn't always freeze at 0°C.
7. Most of the earth's freshwater is underground.
8. Water is the only substance found on earth as a liquid, solid, and gas.
9. The average American uses up to 100 gallons of water a day.
10. Water is the best health tonic that there is.

After everything Jesus went through before and during His crucifixion, it should not be surprising that He was thirsty. Psalm chapter 22 also refers to it.

Psalm 22:15 says, ***"My mouth is dried up like a potsherd, and my tongue sticks to the roof of my mouth; you lay me in the dust of death."***

David again describes something that is not recorded about his own life. He speaks to the future of a time when thirst would be an issue.

A ***"potsherd"*** is a piece of broken pottery. What was once a useful vessel can no longer hold any water. It is clearly dry; no water is found in it.

John Calvin states how this verse describes Jesus' death, *"My strength is dried up.* He means the vigour which is imparted to us by the radical moisture, as physicians call it. What he adds in the next clause, *My tongue cleaveth to my jaws,* is of the same import. We know that excessive grief not only consumes the vital spirits, but also dries up almost all the moisture which is in our bodies."

This basic concept of thirst is recorded and fulfilled in John 19:28-30, **"Later, knowing that everything had now been finished, and so that Scripture would be fulfilled, Jesus said, 'I am thirsty.' A jar of wine vinegar was there, so they soaked a sponge in it, put the sponge on a stalk of the hyssop plant, and lifted it to Jesus' lips. When he had received the drink, Jesus said, 'It is finished.' With that, he bowed his head and gave up his spirit."**

Jesus said, **"I am thirsty."** It sounds so basic, yet it fulfills David's prophecy from Psalm chapter 22. Actually, another prophecy is fulfilled by Jesus by the way those who were crucifying Him responded. Psalm 69:21 says, **"They put gall in my food and gave me vinegar for my thirst."** David is also the author of this Psalm. Jesus was thirsty, and they offered Him vinegar.

Jesus saying He was thirsty can be argued as a way of Him "choosing" to fulfill a prophecy. However, one does not get to choose how others will respond. Not only are we talking about others, but it is those who are killing Him. Not only does it say they will respond to His statement, but it gives how they will respond by giving vinegar. The attention to detail is so precise and encouraging. David was speaking about Jesus in both Psalm chapter 22 and Psalm chapter 69.

It is good to pause for a moment and be reminded that although Jesus was and is God, He became a man. He was also human. He got thirsty.

Bradley W. Matson wisely says, "Were Jesus not humanity He could not relate to us adequately to pay our penalty. Were Jesus not God, the penalty could not be sufficient for all the sins of the world."

Side Note

Psalm 22:15 says, *"My mouth is dried up like a potsherd, and my tongue sticks to the roof of my mouth; you lay me in the dust of death."* This last phrase needs attention. Although I am not using it as a major point, it can be viewed as a Messianic Prophecy (a statement pointing out something about the Messiah who was to come).

Obviously, David is not speaking of his own death. It would be hard for the reader to comprehend that the coming Messiah would be placed *"in the dust of death."* They could only envision a powerful, victorious leader. He was the Savior. His death was not a point of daily discussion.

However, Isaiah 53:9 does refer to the Messiah's death, *"He was assigned a grave with the wicked, and with the rich in his death, though he had done no violence, nor was any deceit in his mouth."* By being assigned a grave, it is clear He was to die. Even though He was innocent, He was to die. We now know it was, and is, for our sins.

Isaiah 53:12 adds, *"Therefore I will give him a portion among the great, and he will divide the spoils with the strong, because he poured out his life unto death, and was numbered with the transgressors. For he bore the sin of many, and made intercession for the transgressors."*

Jesus *"poured out his life unto death"* because *"he bore the sin of many."*

Not only was Jesus thirsty, but He also died. Spoiler alert: He did not stay dead. He rose again!

CHAPTER 8
PIERCED HANDS AND FEET

Dogs surround me,
a pack of villains encircles me;
they pierce my hands and my feet.

Psalm 22:16

Piercings are a pretty commonplace venture in today's culture. It normally involves one or both ears but can become an "addiction" for some as they add more.

Guinness World Records documents the most piercings by a man and a woman. The most pierced man is Rolf Buchholz of Germany, who had 453 piercings (the last count was taken in 2010).

Elaine Davidson of Brazil has a lot more piercings. Within a ten-year span, she was pierced a total of 4,225 times (the last count was taken in 2006). *Guinness World Records* goes on to say, "The former restaurant owner is constantly adding and replacing jewelry, mostly in her face. She enhances her exotic looks with tattoos and brightly colored make-up, and often wears feathers and streamers in her hair."

Even though people today will pierce any and everything between their nose and toes, it is not a new phenomenon. The Bible records that there was piercing, even around 1500 B.C.

Exodus 21:5-6 says, ***"But if the servant declares, 'I love my master and my wife and children and do not want to go free,' then his master must take him before the judges. He shall take him to the door or the door-post and pierce his ear with an awl. Then he will be his servant for life."***

The people could only have a Hebrew slave for six years. They had to let them go in the seventh year. However, if the slave liked the situation, he could become a slave for life. The way to signify this was for him to have his ear pierced.

A pierced ear meant that you have a good master and want to be a slave for life. It is actually the concept that is conveyed in James 1:1 (NKJV), *"James, a bondservant of God and of the Lord Jesus Christ."* The New Living Translation translates this passage as, *"This letter is from James, a slave of God and of the Lord Jesus Christ."*

However, the original readers would have been confused reading Psalm 22:16, *"Dogs surround me, a pack of villains encircles me; they pierce my hands and my feet."*

In chapter four, the concept of the Messiah being surrounded by evil individuals (*"Dogs"*) has already been discussed. Bradley W. Matson adds to the conversation, "Most cities would have vicious, wild, mongrel dogs that would travel in packs around the edge of town. They were dangerous and aggressive. This is the picture of Christ's situation."

The stronger image from this passage is, *"They pierce my hands and my feet."* It is clear that it was not about David, but the crucifixion of Jesus.

As is common knowledge today, but was not in David's time, piercing one's hands and feet is how one would keep the "victim" from falling off the cross.

Although Jesus was crucified and buried, He rose again. He came back to life! He initially appeared to ten of the disciples, but Thomas was not there. John 20:25-29 describes Thomas' response to the news that Jesus was alive, *"So the other disciples told him, 'We have seen the Lord!' But he said to them, 'Unless I see the nail marks in his hands and put my finger where the nails were, and put my hand into his side, I will not believe.' A week later his disciples were in the house again, and Thomas was with them. Though the doors were locked, Jesus came and stood among them and said, 'Peace be with you!' Then he said to Thomas, 'Put your finger here; see my hands. Reach out your hand and put it into my side. Stop doubting and believe.' Thomas said to him, 'My Lord and my God!' Then Jesus told him, 'Because you have seen me, you have believed; blessed are those who have not seen and yet have believed.'"*

Thomas knew Jesus had been crucified and, therefore, would have scars from it. Seeing Jesus alive again radically changed his heart.

This scenario of Psalm chapter 22 describing a crucifixion is so powerful that Rabbis today are trying to change the word "pierced" to "torn." They want to deflect the attention away from Jesus being the Messiah, so they change one Hebrew letter.

David wrote this about 1,000 years before Jesus was crucified. Yet, they try to dispute that 3,000 years later. We know it was at least written 400 years before Jesus because of what is called the "Silent Years." Once God had given details of the coming of the Messiah, He did not speak with man for 400 years. This is the intermission time between the Old Testament and the New Testament. If that sounds too confusing, there is one major problem for the Rabbis who are trying to change any word. It is the Septuagint.

In 250 BC, 70 Jewish priests translated the Hebrew Old Testament into Greek. The word they read was "pierced." This was "Jewish priests" meticulously translating each Hebrew word into Greek. The passage had to exist to be translated, and the word was pierced. Because it was 70 Jewish priests, the Septuagint is often simply referred to as LXX.

John Calvin pointed out that Jews changed the word for pierced after the Septuagint was written to turn people from looking to Jesus on the cross and acknowledging Him as the Messiah and Redeemer.

Side Note

Not only does Psalm 22:16 use the word "pierced," but so does Zechariah 12:10, *"And I will pour out on the house of David and the inhabitants of Jerusalem a spirit of grace and supplication. They will look on me, the one they have pierced, and they will mourn for him as one mourns for an only child, and grieve bitterly for him as one grieves for a firstborn son."* It is difficult for Rabbis to accept that the Messiah would need to be pierced and die.

Not only were Jesus' hands and feet pierced, but the soldiers also pierced His side. John 19:33-37 records the event, *"But when they came to Jesus and found that he was already dead, they did not break his legs. Instead, one of the soldiers pierced Jesus' side with a spear, bringing a sudden flow of blood and water. The man who saw it has given testimony, and his testimony is true. He knows that he tells the truth, and he testifies so that you also may believe. These things happened so that the scripture would be fulfilled: 'Not one of his bones will be broken,' and, as another scripture says, 'They will look on the one they have pierced.'"* John actually quotes the Zechariah passage to help connect the dots for his readers.

Zechariah said the Messiah would be pierced. John pointed out that Jesus was pierced to fulfill the prophecy. It may seem overly obvious, but Jesus did not "choose" or "make" the soldiers pierce His side after He was dead. Everything points to Jesus being the Messiah.

That the Messiah would be "pierced" is also foretold in Isaiah 53:5, *"But he was pierced for our transgressions, he was crushed for our iniquities; the punishment that brought us peace was on him, and by his wounds we are healed."* Our relationship with God was broken due to our sin. This relationship was healed by Jesus' death.

CHAPTER 9

NO BROKEN BONES

All my bones are on display;
people stare and gloat over me.
Psalm 22:17

There are 206 bones in the human body. Evel Knievel (Robert Craig Knievel) was known as a daredevil as he would ride his motorcycle jumping from ramp to ramp over various obstacles. Of his 150 appearances, he "crashed" on 18 of them resulting in 433 fractures of 35 different bones. He fractured his skull, nose, jaw, both collarbones, both arms, both wrists, his sternum, every single rib, his back five times, both ankles, some toes, his right shin, right knee, tailbone, left hip, and had his pelvis crushed and broken three times. He often focused on setting new records and in the process, set the record for most broken bones.

Even though Jesus was crucified, none of His bones were broken. This aligns with the Old Testament. Psalm 22:17 says, *"All my bones are on display; people stare and gloat over me."* Jesus' bones were easy to see, but none of them were broken.

It is important that none of Jesus' bones were broken for at least two reasons. First, this fulfilled prophecy. Psalm 34:20 adds, *"He protects all his bones, not one of them will be broken."* While Psalm chapter 22 might hint at the fact, Psalm chapter 34 is very straight forward that none of the Messiah's bones would be broken.

The second reason it is important that none of Jesus' bones were broken is that Jesus' death correlates with the guidelines for the Passover found in Exodus chapter 12.

Not only were the Israelites celebrating when God delivered them from Egypt by "passing over" their houses due to the blood of the lamb on the door, but it also pointed forward to the Messiah.

As they prepared for the Passover meal, they had specific instructions. Exodus 12:46 says, *"It must be eaten inside the house; take none of the meat outside the house. Do not break any of the bones."* Numbers 9:12 adds, *"They must not leave any of it till morning or break any of its bones. When they celebrate the Passover, they must follow all the regulations."* It was clear that none of the bones of the lamb were to be broken.

Knowing this helps one understand a specific title for Jesus. John 1:29 says, *"The next day John saw Jesus coming towards him and said, 'Look, the Lamb of God, who takes away the sin of the world!'"* Jesus was called *"the Lamb of God"* because instead of covering a few sins, He came to take *"away the sin of the world!"* Later, John again refers to Jesus as *"the Lamb of God"* (John 1:36).

This concept of Jesus being referred to as a lamb is also stated in 1 Peter 1:18-19, *"For you know that it was not with perishable things such as silver or gold that you were redeemed from the empty way of life handed down to you from your ancestors, but with the precious blood of Christ, a lamb without blemish or defect."* The book of Revelation also references Jesus as the Lamb (Revelation 6:16; 12:11; 17:14; 21:27; 22:3).

When someone was crucified, their legs were often broken to speed up the death process. With broken legs, they would not be able to push up with their legs to lessen the stress on the lungs.

John 19:31-37 describes how even though Jesus was crucified, His bones were not broken, *"Now it was the day of Preparation, and the next day was to be a special Sabbath. Because the Jewish leaders did not want the bodies left on the crosses during the Sabbath, they asked Pilate to have the legs broken and the bodies taken down. The soldiers therefore came and broke the legs of the first man who had been crucified with Jesus, and then those of the other. But when they came to Jesus and found that he was already dead, they did not break his legs. Instead, one of the soldiers pierced Jesus' side with a spear, bringing a sudden flow of blood and water. The man who saw it has given testimony, and his testimony is true. He knows that he tells the truth, and he testifies so that you also may believe. These things happened so that the scripture would be fulfilled: 'Not one of his bones will be broken,' and, as another scripture says, 'They will look on the one they have pierced.'"*

None of the Messiah's bones were to be broken; none of Jesus' bones were broken. Psalm chapter 22 describes the crucifixion of Jesus. The prophecy concerning the Messiah is well documented. Jesus fulfilled all of them. There are over 300 prophecies concerning the Messiah. If Jesus fails on even one account, He is disqualified. Anything less than 100% was a failure. Jesus is the Messiah, the Savior, the Lamb of God.

Psalm chapter 22 is a song of praise.

CHAPTER 10
CAST LOTS FOR CLOTHING

They divide my clothes among them
and cast lots for my garment.
Psalm 22:18

In 2013, Karl Smallwood wrote an article entitled, *"The 4 Most Childish Ways Powerful People Settled Arguments."* The four examples are quite amazing.

1. Southwest Airlines created a slogan ("Just Plane Smart"), not realizing it infringed on Stevens Aviation's slogan. Instead of going to court, Stevens Aviation CEO Kurt Herwald challenged rival CEO Herb Kelleher to an arm-wrestling match. The winner got to keep the slogan.

2. A Japanese businessman, Takashi Hashiyama, had an expensive art collection he decided to sell. He was not sure whether to use Sotheby's or Christie's auction house. He decided to have them settle the matter between themselves. They played "Rock, Paper, Scissors."

3. British law states that if an election ends in a tie, they draw straws to settle the tie. They do not have a recount or vote again. They just draw straws, and whoever has the longer straw wins.

4. In 1845, Frances Pettygrove (from Portland, Maine) and Asa Lovejoy (from Boston, Massachusetts) owned an area named "The Clearing." Both men wanted to rename the area after their respective hometowns. They decided to flip a coin to determine who gets to decide. Pettygrove won best two out of three and named the area Portland, Oregon.

Arm wrestling, "Rock, Paper, Scissors," drawing straws, and flipping a coin are commonly used ways of coming to a decision. Psalm chapter 22 describes a scenario that was precisely played out as Jesus hung on the cross.

Psalm 22:18 says, *"They divide my clothes among them and cast lots for my garment."* This prophecy would be fulfilled by the enemies of the Messiah. They took His clothes and decided to cast lots for the last seamless piece of clothing.

All four Gospels describe this event with John taking it further by describing it as a fulfillment of Scripture (John 19:23–24; Matthew 27:35; Mark 15:24; Luke 23:34).

John 19:23-24 says, *"When the soldiers crucified Jesus, they took his clothes, dividing them into four shares, one for each of them, with the undergarment remaining. This garment was seamless, woven in one piece from top to bottom. 'Let's not tear it,' they said to one another. 'Let's decide by lot who will get it.' This happened that the scripture might be fulfilled that said, 'They divided my clothes among them and cast lots for my garment.' So this is what the soldiers did."* God chose to use His enemies to fulfill His prophecy. Some of the prophecies Jesus chose to say and do, but other ways needed outside action. The people who did not view Jesus as the Messiah helped prove He was and is.

Willem VanGemeren adds, "The enemies are described by their hostile activities and also portrayed by metaphors. The enemies are likened to a multitude of 'strong bulls' (v. 12), to 'roaring lions' (v. 13; cf. v. 21), to 'dogs' (vv. 16, 20), and to 'wild oxen' (v. 21). The enemies are all around (vv. 12, 16), making disturbing sounds (v. 13) and rejoicing over his misery (vv. 16–18)." Yet, they help fulfill the prophecy. It is actually quite comical.

Imagine this scene: Jesus is on the cross. He has been speaking in Greek, and everyone basically understands what He is saying. However, He changes directions and starts speaking in Arabic as He quotes Psalm chapter 22 (and possibly the whole chapter), *"My God, my God, why have you forsaken me?"* As the Jewish men are singing, humming, or thinking through the Psalm, I wonder if the soldiers were dividing the garments just as they came to verse 18. Did everyone immediately look at the soldiers? Did the soldiers get that eerie feeling that people were staring at them? They do not understand the language. The Jewish men are seeing prophecy being fulfilled, and those dividing the clothes cannot understand what is being said and why everyone has a startled look on their faces.

God created humor and knows the power of timing. It is possible and maybe probable that He may have done everything exactly that way.

They did not arm wrestle, play "Rock, Paper, Scissors," draw straws, or flip a coin for His clothes. A soldier did not just grab the clothes and tear them or run off with them. No, they cast lots for His clothing.

CHAPTER 11
ONLY SON

Deliver me from the sword,
my precious life from the power of the dogs.
Psalm 22:20

In May 2018, Tetiana Vasylenko wrote an interesting article entitled, *"Small funny translation mistakes that have caused serious problems."* She lists five company slogan translations that did not go well for their business in the other country.

1. Pepsi - In the 1960s, Pepsi's slogan was, "Come alive with the Pepsi generation." Unfortunately, as they were breaking into the Chinese market, the slogan translated into Chinese saying, "Pepsi brings your relatives back from the dead." Needless to say, this translation blunder lost Pepsi a lot of business in China.

2. Kentucky Fried Chicken - KFC's famous slogan "Finger-lickin' good" also became a hilarious phrase in China. When translated into Chinese, the slogan became twisted as, "Eat your fingers off." Not quite what we mean when we refer to finger food.

3. Coors – The Famous American beer maker had a tagline, "Turn it loose." It was translated into Spanish as "suffer from diarrhea." The slogan worked as the Spanish customers did notice the brand, but not for the right reason.

4. Schweppes – This popular beverage brand faced a really inconvenient situation in Italy. The tagline of its brand, "Schweppes Tonic Water," became "Schweppes Toilet Water" in Italian. Maybe a fun prank gift, but not great for sales.

5. General Electric - When GE decided to make its way into Europe and develop a new partnership, it got a new name, "GPT." However, "GPT" in French is pronounced as "J'ai pete," meaning "I farted." That would be a creative way to create energy, but obviously, that was not the plan.

In Psalm chapter 22, there is a verse where how one translates a word can make for another powerful point. Psalm 22:20 says, **"Deliver me from the sword, my precious life from the power of the dogs."**

"Precious life" in Hebrew is a single word (יְחִיד - pronounced yachid) and can be translated as "only, only one, solitary, lonely, one and child, only son" *(New American Standard Hebrew-Aramaic and Greek dictionaries)*. In the *Dictionary of Biblical Languages with Semantic Domains: Hebrew,* James Swanson adds more insight to the translation meaning by saying, "Only unique child, i.e., pertaining to a child very special in the eyes of the parent, and in that sense unique."

The New International Version (NIV) and English Standard Version (ESV) translate "yachid" as **"precious life."** It is interesting to see how other common translations interpret this word. The New American Standard Bible (NASB) says, **"only life."** The King James Version (KJV) says, **"darling."** The New King James Version says, **"life."** All of these translations are accurate and acceptable.

Charles Spurgeon referred to Psalm 22:20 (KJV) when he said, "My darling had better be rendered 'my lonely, or solitary one.'"

"Yachid" is also found in Proverbs 4:3, **"For I too was a son to my father, still tender, and cherished by my mother."** The New International Version translates the word as **"cherished."** It is also translated as **"only one"** (ESV), **"only son"** (NASB), and **"only beloved"** (KJV). The emphasis is that there is a special bond associated with this son.

This clearly is not talking about David as 1 Chronicles 2:13-15 explains, *"Jesse was the father of Eliab his firstborn; the second son was Abinadab, the third Shimea, the fourth Nethanel, the fifth Raddai, the sixth Ozem and the seventh David."* David had at least six brothers.

The *"only son"* is not referring to David, but the Messiah. It is noteworthy that when the Hebrew is transferred into Greek, it uses the same word that we find in John 3:16, *"For God so loved the world that he gave his one and only Son, that whoever believes in him shall not perish but have eternal life."* Jesus is the *"one and only Son,"* referred to in John 3:16 and Psalm 22:20.

Of further interest, The *Gesenius' Hebrew and Chaldee Lexicon to the Old Testament Scriptures* says *"precious life"* can be interpreted as "only, especially only begotten, only child." Again, it is clear from the King James Version who this is talking about, *"For God so loved the world, that he gave his only begotten Son, that whosoever believeth in him should not perish, but have everlasting life"* (John 3:16).

Zechariah 12:10 connects the *"only child"* translation with the concept of this son being *"pierced."* It says, *"And I will pour out on the house of David and the inhabitants of Jerusalem a spirit of grace and supplication. They will look on me, the one they have pierced, and they will mourn for him as one mourns for an only child, and grieve bitterly for him as one grieves for a firstborn son."*

Jesus is the *"only begotten son"* who was *"pierced"* in our place and for our sin. Praise should be given for this *"precious life."*

Side Note

In his book, *Opening Up Psalms,* Roger Ellsworth understands that Psalm chapter 22 is not talking about David but the coming Messiah. He makes an interesting distinction in the direction of the Psalm, "The psalm falls into two easily discernible sections. The first is the Messiah's description of the crucifixion (verses 1–21a). The second is his description of the results of the crucifixion (verses 21b–31). We might say the psalm is divided between the Messiah's experience on the cross and his exultation in the results of the cross."

Psalm chapter 22 does describe the crucifixion of Jesus the Christ, but it also goes on to say what that means to us. David's death had no impact on our lives, but Jesus' death brings victory.

Duane Garrett wrote, *"The Poetic and Wisdom Books,"* in which he gives a concise summary of Psalm chapter 22, "The triumphant conclusion is unusually long. David's situation is a type of the sufferings and resurrection of Christ. The psalm anticipates Christ's outcry from the cross (Matt. 27:46), the mockery He received (Luke 23:35), His pain and thirst (John 19:28), the piercing of His hands and feet, and the casting of lots for His clothes (John 19:23–24). But it also looks forward to His victory and the coming of people from all nations to submit to Him." Victory comes in following Jesus.

Jesus sang on the cross. It was and is a song of victory for those who choose to follow Him.

CHAPTER 12
GOD AND GOD

For he has not despised or scorned
the suffering of the afflicted one;
he has not hidden his face from him but has
listened to his cry for help.
From you comes the theme of my praise
in the great assembly; before those who fear you
I will fulfil my vows.
The poor will eat and be satisfied; those who seek
the Lord will praise him – may your hearts live
forever!

Psalm 22:24-26

"I wanted to do what was best for LeBron James, and what LeBron James was going to do to make him happy." This quote sounds quite basic until one realizes it was said by LeBron James in a 2010 TV interview. He is speaking of himself in the third person.

An elementary refresher would remind us that first, second, and the third person are ways of describing points of view. The first person is the "I" or "we" perspective. The second person is the "you" perspective. The third person is the "he," "she," "it," or "they" perspective. One normally does not refer to themselves in the third person.

When a statement refers to oneself in the third person instead of the first person, it is officially called an "illeism." This style of speech or writing can be intentional to provide emphasis on a certain thought.

In Psalm 22:24-26, it can be valuable to follow the pronoun trail, *"For he has not despised or scorned the suffering of the afflicted one; he has not hidden his face from him but has listened to his cry for help. From you comes the theme of my praise in the great assembly; before those who fear you I will fulfil my vows. The poor will eat and be satisfied; those who seek the Lord will praise him – may your hearts live forever!"* Which pronouns refer to the Lord?

This can be confusing or explained by the doctrine of the Trinity (the Father, Son, and Holy Spirit are all One, and are all God). David seems to understand who the Lord is as he makes the same kind of statement in Psalm 110:1, *"The Lord says to my lord: 'Sit at my right hand until I make your enemies a footstool for your feet.'"*

Clearly, Psalm chapter 22 is not an autobiography written by David. He is expressing in amazing detail the struggles and events that happened at the Crucifixion of the Messiah, Jesus.

The Bible is amazing in how it speaks in detail of things that happened 1,000 years later.

Side Note

It is encouraging to see Psalm chapter 22 move from a picture of the Lord being abused and despised and move to an element of praise. Psalm 22:26 ends with the phrase, ***"hearts live forever!"***

How could David's life and death ever bring a concept of eternal life? It could not, and it did not, but Jesus' life and death have.

The question of the Kingdom of God and eternal life was raised by a rich man in Matthew 19:16, ***"Just then a man came up to Jesus and asked, 'Teacher, what good thing must I do to get eternal life?'"*** It was a fair question. It is a question that should be asked by everyone today.

The answer is clearly seen in several Bible verses.

John 3:16 is one of the most famous verses of the Bible because it simply says, ***"For God so loved the world that he gave his one and only Son, that whoever believes in him shall not perish but have eternal life."*** God loved us, so He sent His Son to die for us (crucifixion). This puts us at a point of choice. Follow Jesus and have eternal life (Heaven) or stay in our own ways and perish (Hell). There are two eternal destinations. God does not want anyone to perish, but He also does not want to "force" people to love Him.

John 3:36 adds, *"Whoever believes in the Son has eternal life, but whoever rejects the Son will not see life, for God's wrath remains on them."* The concept of *"hearts live forever"* is not positive for the one who rejects Jesus. God's wrath will be on him.

John 5:24 says, *"Very truly I tell you, whoever hears my word and believes him who sent me has eternal life and will not be judged but has crossed over from death to life."* Eternal life is promised for the one who believes in Jesus.

An easy verse to memorize on this truth is John 6:47, *"Very truly I tell you, the one who believes has eternal life."*

Romans 6:23 addresses the "cost" issue, *"For the wages of sin is death, but the gift of God is eternal life in Christ Jesus our Lord."* Some translations even call eternal life a *"free gift."* The redundancy emphasizes that although it cost Jesus His life, it is free to us.

This promise is something that we can be confident about because 1 John 5:11-13 tells us, *"And this is the testimony: God has given us eternal life, and this life is in his Son. Whoever has the Son has life; whoever does not have the Son of God does not have life. I write these things to you who believe in the name of the Son of God so that you may know that you have eternal life."* God wants His followers confident in His love. He has written everything plainly so we can *"know that you have eternal life."*

The concepts of *"hearts live forever"* and *"eternal life"* are both born out of the sacrifice seen in the crucifixion of Jesus. Psalm chapter 22 brings the story of Jesus' death as part of

His mission by showing years earlier that this would allow hearts to live forever.

David knew eternal life came to *"those who seek the Lord"* (Psalm 22:26).

Side Note

Jesus said, *"My God, my God, why have you forsaken me?"* This was not because He was forsaken by the Father. It was to draw the audiences' attention to Psalm chapter 22.

Psalm 22:24 shows that God was always present, *"For he has not despised or scorned the suffering of the afflicted one; he has not hidden his face from him but has listened to his cry for help."*

Instead of abandonment, God was present. He did not hide His face from His Son.

Please understand, God will not hide from you. Hebrews 13:5 comforts us, *"Keep your lives free from the love of money and be content with what you have, because God has said, 'Never will I leave you; never will I forsake you.'"* God will never turn His back on His children.

CHAPTER 13
IT IS FINISHED

They will proclaim his righteousness,
declaring to a people yet unborn:
He has done it!
Psalm 22:31

The tallest church in the world will be Sagrada Família. It is a beautiful church in Barcelona, Spain. However, it is not finished yet.

Construction began in 1882, but it is not finished. The famous architect Antoni Gaudí dedicated himself to finishing it until his death in 1926. Actually, in 2010, reports say it was only halfway finished. The optimistic goal is to finish by the year 2026 (100 years after the passing of Gaudí).

Gaudí worked on the church for about 44 years. Can you imagine how many generations could have been involved? If we consider a new generation every 20 years, there could already be about ten generations. A man or woman could work on building a church their great, great, great, great, great, great, great, great, and great grandfather helped build.

Imagine the feeling when it is finally finished.

People get excited over finishing a 2,000-piece puzzle, a long novel, a spring clean of the garage, or their toddler eating all their vegetables. Finishing something can be exciting, but taking on a life-long project has so much more depth.

Psalm 22:31 says, *"They will proclaim his righteousness, declaring to a people yet unborn: He has done it!"*

As this Psalm is being wrapped up, David says, *"He has done it!"* This Psalm is for *"a people yet unborn."* It is not about David's life, but a future time. It is about the Messiah, who will be known for finishing a life-long mission. It will be done; He will have conquered all odds. Everything was completed to the most precise detail.

It can bring chills when one combines this passage with John 19:30, *"When he had received the drink, Jesus said, 'It is finished.' With that, he bowed his head and gave up his spirit."*

Miles Custis wrote, "The final line — which consists of one word in Hebrew — can be translated either 'he has done it' or simply 'it is done.' Jesus may be alluding to this when he says — with one word in Greek — 'it is finished' (John 19:30). Christ's dying words carry many implications: God's plan of salvation has been completed; our sin is paid for; Christ's work on earth is done. Perhaps it is also a shout of praise like the psalmist's words in Psalm 22:31. It is finished. God's ultimate deliverance has been carried out."

Richard Patterson is credited with pointing out that the Greek word in John 19:30 (*"it is finished"*) alludes to the Hebrew word in Psalm 22:31 (*"He has done it"*). Furthermore, when the Hebrew Old Testament was translated into the Greek (called the Septuagint), the word for *"it is finished"* was often used (Nehemiah 6:16; Isaiah 55:11).

Many theologians believe Jesus most likely quoted all of Psalm chapter 22 in Aramaic for His Jewish audience as they watched it played out before their very eyes. Ed Rickard even wrote, "When Jesus finally came to the end of the psalm, He shouted out the words, 'It is finished.'"

Charles Spurgeon adds, "It may have been actually repeated word by word by our Lord when hanging on the tree." Jesus finished quoting Psalm chapter 22, took one more breath (or gasped for one more breath), and said, *"It is finished!"*

It is possible (and maybe probable) that right after Jesus finished quoting Psalm chapter 22 or the people completed making the connection between what they were seeing and what they had memorized (*"He has done it"*) that Jesus said, *"It is finished!"* That is the ultimate "mic drop."

It should be noticed that Psalm chapter 22 references three statements from the cross:

1. *"My God, my God, why have you forsaken me?"*
2. *"I Thirst."*
3. *"It is finished!"*

David knew that when the Messiah would come, He would finish what needed to be done for us. Jesus finished His mission.

2 Timothy 4:7 challenges us, *"I have fought the good fight, I have finished the race, I have kept the faith."* We, too, need to finish strong and complete what God has called us to do.

CHAPTER 13: IT IS FINISHED

CONCLUSION

In 1998, the Detroit Red Wings hockey team qualified for the playoffs. Expectations are always high in "Hockeytown." Detroit was the defending Stanley Cup champions. Detroit beat the Phoenix Coyotes in the first round four games to two. However, the second round was against the rival St. Louis Blues.

Detroit and St. Louis split the first two games, and fortunately, Detroit won game three in double overtime. Detroit won game four but lost game five at home. It was a frustrating loss, and they were headed to St. Louis. They were losing momentum.

Something happened between games five and six that changed the direction of the playoffs. The story has it that an assistant coach from St. Louis accidentally left his playbook at the hotel in Detroit. Hotel management contacted the Red Wing organization and gave them the prized playbook. Everything was kept secretive.

Detroit management studied the playbook and created a fabulous game plan. The Red Wings went into St. Louis with a new found confidence. St. Louis ended up singing the "blues" as they got pounded six goals to one.

Detroit went on to beat the Dallas Stars and swept the Washington Capitals in the Stanley Cup Finals. The Detroit Red Wings were champs again.

Even if the story cannot be verified, having the other team's playbook can be very helpful. God's Word is our playbook. God has let His enemy, Satan, have full access to it. Satan has studied it but cannot change the outcome.

CONCLUSION

Satan knows what the Bible says. He knows what God is going to do. He cannot do anything about changing God's plan. God wins!

A study of Psalm chapter 22 shows that the Bible is trustworthy. It cannot be changed or altered. It will not fail. The Bible (as has been shown from Psalm chapter 22) records numerous prophecies of the Messiah, which are clearly fulfilled in Jesus.

Can we trust the Bible? Absolutely!

The Bible is unique, powerful, and beautiful. It is written to protect us and provide for us. It is God-breathed and sharper than any two-edged sword. It accurately records the past, present, and future. Some of the prophecies have already been fulfilled, and some are yet to come.

The Bible also gives some commonsense advice:

- Do not go to bed angry.
- Do not be anxious about anything.
- Praying is healthier than stressing.
- Silver rule – "Do not do something to someone else if you do not want it done to you."
- Golden rule – "Do to others what you would want to be done to you."

Finally, the Bible is a love letter. God created us and wanted to have a relationship with us. We turned our back on Him. Sin broke that relationship. God still loved us, so He sent His Son to come to Earth, live a perfect life, and die in our place for our sins. Although He was placed in a tomb, He rose again. He is alive and offers us eternal life by His grace. It is a gift. It can not be bought or earned. We receive it through faith.

God says, *"If you declare with your mouth, 'Jesus is Lord,' and believe in your heart that God raised him from the dead, you will be saved. For, 'everyone who calls on the name of the Lord will be saved'"* (Romans 10:9, 13).

CONCLUSION